SIMPLE

Organizing

MELISSA MICHAELS

HARVEST HOUSE PUBLISHERS
EUGENE, OREGON

Cover design by Nicole Dougherty
Cover Image © Inna Ogando / Shutterstock
Interior design by Paul Nielsen, Faceoutstudio
Kids' room photos by Cassie Kulp (cassiekulp.com)

Published in association with William K. Jensen Literary Agency

SIMPLE ORGANIZING

Copyright © 2018 Melissa Michaels
Published by Harvest House Publishers
Eugene, Oregon 97408
www.harvesthousepublishers.com

ISBN 978-0-7369-6315-2 (pbk.)
ISBN 978-0-7369-6316-9 (eBook)

Library of Congress Catalog-in-Publication Data
Names: Michaels, Melissa, author.
Title: Simple organizing / Melissa Michaels.
Description: Eugene, Oregon : Harvest House Publishers, [2018] | Includes
   bibliographical references.
Identifiers: LCCN 2017034555 (print) | LCCN 2017039053 (ebook) | ISBN
   9780736963169 (ebook) | ISBN 9780736963152 (pbk.)
Subjects: LCSH: Housekeeping. | Orderliness.
Classification: LCC TX301 (ebook) | LCC TX301 .M49 2018 (print) | DDC
   648—dc23
LC record available at https://lccn.loc.gov/2017034555

Printed in China

18 19 20 21 22 23 24 25 26 / RDS-FO / 10 9 8 7 6 5 4 3 2 1

Contents

MAKE THE MOST
OF YOUR SPACE

Your home is your special place to live life. Whether you're living in your dream home or a small apartment, the same rule should apply to getting yourself organized: Make the most of the space you have.

Organization isn't just about setting up a storage system. It's about designing a home that truly reflects your family. By using pieces that are pleasing to your eye, you'll actually *enjoy* maintaining your space. The systems you select become a way to showcase your style and keep your home under control at the same time.

Best of all, as you organize your home, you also organize your life. You don't waste time searching for missing items. Your surfaces are clearer, so your mind feels clearer too. You're not afraid to entertain friends or neighbors. Your home won't be perfect, but that's okay. That's not the point. It will be presentable and comfortable and a place you're proud to call your own.

Tip: You can motivate yourself to further cleaning and decluttering by taking before-and-after photographs of your newly cleaned and organized area. Even if it isn't perfect, progress inspires!

As we journey through the spaces of our homes, beginning with the entryway, you'll begin to catch a vision of the best organizing plan for you and your loved ones. You may feel most at home with lots of empty space and room to breathe. Or you may be content with a cozy amount of treasures, wanting to be surrounded by a comfortable amount of stuff. No matter your preference, you'll learn to look at your home with a practiced eye, determining what you truly use and what you could do without.

After you've cleared the clutter, you can establish some simple habits and routines that keep your home—and your life—well ordered and organized. Simple organizing is about making the most of the space you have and creating a home that works for your family so you can get on to the most important things in life! The things that aren't *things* at all. That's the heart behind simple organizing.

Entrances

Entrances

SET THE STAGE FOR A WELCOMING HOME

When you visit homes you love, what do you feel as soon as you step into the entryway? What says welcome? What do you want your guests—as well as those who live in your home—to feel when they step into your entryway?

The entryway sets the tone for the rest of your home. You can ascertain a feeling of calm or chaos right from the start. A tiny entryway can look larger with the right organizing plan, and even a large entryway can appear cluttered when there's too much stuff in the mix.

Entrances also dictate the tone of our coming and going. If coats and backpacks and keys are easy to access, we can head out the door with a positive attitude. But if we're scrambling to find important papers and searching for a matching shoe, we're not going to start off our day on the right foot. Maybe even literally!

With simple storage solutions and a look at the big picture, the entryway can set the stage for a feeling of order in the rest of the home. No remodels or renovations are necessary to get organized. Use what you have—that's a theme throughout this book—and make the most of your space. That's the best way to create a warm welcome.

1 | START SMART

Take a look around your home. Do your spaces look tidy, organized, and welcoming? Or do clutter and chaos take center stage? Don't worry if you answered "clutter and chaos." You're not alone.

Every day we make choices that contribute to disorder in our homes. We put things down instead of putting them away. We fail to create designated spaces for our stuff. We put off picking up until the next day—and then we run out of time. And that's okay. We can't expect perfection every single day.

When you're not sure what to do first, set just one goal. When you're feeling wishy-washy or indecisive about what to do next, take one specific step. I recommend starting in your entryway—the space that visitors (and you and your family!) see when you first walk into your house. Then choose just one thing to improve or organize. It might be a pile of discarded shoes or a stack of mail or all the stuff you need to walk your dog.

You'll be successful in your organizing if you remember to let go of the perfect solution and commit to just a simple one. A foolproof way to do this is by setting goals that are SMART:

S—Specific: Get rid of the pile of shoes cluttering up the entry instead of simply lining them up over and over again.

M—Measurable: Pare down what is kept in this space, allowing only one pair of shoes per family member to be left in the entry.

A—Achievable: Find a storage system so you can keep the shoes in the entry but allow them to stay hidden.

R—Realistic: Don't set an unnecessary goal, such as designing an elaborate shoe storage system for multiple pairs of shoes per person. Fewer shoes and less mess in the entry is the goal, not more storage for more stuff.

T—Time Limited: Set a timeline for steps and completion, such as 30 minutes in the morning or afternoon.

Start with the entryway—and start SMART. Make a series of small, simple goals to kick out the chaos and get your home simply organized.

2

FASHION A FABULOUS FRONT PORCH

First impressions. Curb appeal. Opening statement. If you're accustomed to entering your house through the garage or back door, you might not realize the impact your front porch makes on your entire home. Pop onto your porch and take a critical look. Is the Christmas wreath still up—and you're midway through February? Is the main focal point a massive mountain of kids' toys? Are empty pots or broken planters cluttering up valuable gathering space?

Prioritize organizing your front porch and giving your family and friends a little more room and reason to linger when the weather is nice. It's pretty incredible what eliminating excess clutter can do for adding a welcoming vibe. Even if your porch looks more like a small stoop, you can add curb appeal and function.

CLEAN SWEEP

The best way to bring order to your porch? Get everything off it—plants, furniture, kids' toys, mats, storage boxes. Sweep it clean (including around the frame of the front door), eliminate the cobwebs, scrub the house numbers, hose everything off, and get it looking like new. Then assess what you *truly* want to put back. Chances are you'll love how sparkling the empty space looks and won't be willing to return every item.

FEET FIRST

Either clean your front porch mat of all mud, dirt, and leaves, or splurge on a new one if the old one is beyond help. Fun patterns and styles can be found inexpensively at discount stores. You can even change them up to match the season.

TOY TAMER

While kids should be encouraged to play outdoors and provided with the necessary equipment, scattered toys can really ruin the look. Corral front yard toys in a big basket or bucket. Kids are capable of putting toys away if you provide simple instructions combined with an age-appropriate organizational system.

DOUBLE DUTY

Consider using simple benches or weatherproof outdoor furniture, such as an old table, vintage desk, crate, or unique shelving unit to add storage space for plants, decorative accents, or even creative shoe storage. Super functional and super cute!

SIMPLIFIED SEASONS

While decorating for the holidays is fun, it's easy to go overboard and not be able to keep up with it through the seasons. Give yourself permission to decorate your porch simply. Focus on natural decor you can enjoy for several months, such as potted plants or a simple wreath. A seasonal item or two can be gorgeous when displayed on your front porch and then composted or gotten rid of easily and without guilt when the season is over.

3

WELCOME YOURSELF
LIKE A GUEST

When you walk through your front door multiple times each day, it's easy to not really see your house at all. You're thinking about the meal that needs to be prepared or the meeting you just had or the carpool you're scheduled to pick up.

Next time you come home, step into your entryway and look around. Ask yourself, *How would a guest feel if they were entering my home right now? Does the atmosphere feel chaotic or calm?* Treat your entry like a welcoming haven for yourself and for your family. Make it your favorite place to return to every day!

Realize that the impression you make in the entryway sets the impression for the rest of your house. What does your entry say about your home?

Focus on function. My family's home is happy, casual, and lively. Our small entry is designed to welcome people and pups alike. We keep our home streamlined but casual and informal. Organize your entryway to reflect your family, activities, and interests.

Simplify your stuff. Take five or ten minutes to note what doesn't belong. You can even grab a box or basket and start the decluttering process right then and there. Don't toss the box in the spare bedroom. Give unnecessary things away or recycle.

Think simple, attractive, and organized. A place for everything. What are your needs? Stylish baskets and aesthetically pleasing storage containers can transform a formerly disorderly space. Use what you have or shop in your own home for furniture and organizers to solve storage dilemmas.

Embrace the space you have. Even if you don't have a separate entryway, you can add hooks, a mirror, a rug, or a small bookcase near the door to create a feeling of a designated area. Shuffle things around until it seems just right.

4

ESTABLISH AN ENTRY-LEVEL PLAN

Create a simple checklist you want to tackle so you can stay focused.

Choose a few daily tasks to keep the entry looking fresh and welcoming even during the craziest of weeks. Five fast minutes of sweeping, tidying, and dusting can actually make an amazing difference. If you can't tidy your entry in a matter of minutes, it's time to reevaluate your systems and come up with an easier plan.

Make it your mantra to put things away instead of putting them down. That takes a little more energy, but it will save you valuable minutes in the long run. Bonus: No time wasted tracking down missing items.

Look for the little things—keys, purses, pet leashes, phones, papers. These items tend to scatter and disappear. Designate easy-to-maintain spots for them. Look for trays, baskets, or hooks for your most-used items.

Plan a time during the week for returning everything to its proper place. Turn on some energetic music and get the entire family involved. Or even better, tidy as you go each day. Set up a plan and stick with it. Don't let clutter land and multiply.

Embrace the domino effect: Each positive organizing choice you make, no matter how small or seemingly inconsequential (such as hanging your keys on a hook every time you walk in the door), leads to new, positive choices and actions throughout the day. Make systems easy and practical so everyone in the family can learn to do the same.

Remember that it takes just one wrong decision to start things moving toward disorganization and clutter. A constantly growing pile of shoes, a stack of unopened mail, gloves and scarves tossed on a table...messes like these tend to spill out to other areas of your home.

Add seasonal style to your plan. It's fun to use seasonal decor in the entry-way—a vase of sunflowers in August, a few mini pumpkins in October, tulips in April. Using items from nature works well to reduce clutter because these decorations are temporary and don't need to be stored anywhere. Bonus: A pretty vase or vessel on an entry table can remind you to commit to keeping surfaces clear of clutter.

5 | STRAIGHTEN UP A SMALL SPACE

No matter if your entryway is its own separate room or just the front of your living room, easy storage options help you make the most of this limited area. If you don't have a designated coat closet or enough room for everything you need to access, here are some practical ways to house necessities in a small space.

1. **Lidded boxes, baskets, and small trunks.** Search flea markets, garage sales, or your own closets for useful and pleasing storage options that hide piles of shoes, shopping bags, and winter essentials (such as scarves, hats, and gloves). A tall, open basket or metal container can make it easy to grab an umbrella on the way out the door.

2. **Small trays and bins.** Corral small wayward items—mail, school papers, items to return—in an attractive way. Small trays and bins can keep surfaces or shelves tidy.

3. **Expand your storage.** If your entryway doesn't have enough space for what you need, look for nearby options in adjoining spaces. A dresser in the living room, a guest room closet, or a linen cabinet in a hall can be repurposed as entryway storage space.

4. **Pet-gear crate.** If you're a dog owner like me, you know it's important to have access to going-for-a-walk gear, such as raincoats (yes, our dogs have raincoats for rainy days), harnesses, or flashlights for night-time walks.

5. **The perfect piece.** Furniture can streamline storage for so many entry-way necessities. Look for a shallow cabinet, a small dresser, a slim table with storage below, or a bench with storage or coat rack above.

6. **Creative hangers.** Create more space by getting things up and out of the way. Fashion an original coat hanger for your wall with just about anything (shutters, an old door, a weathered plank of wood) and a few functional, attractive hooks. Remember, hangers aren't just for coats. They're also great for bags, scarves, totes, purses, and anything else that needs a home up and out of the way.

6 | PREP YOUR PURSE

When you're busy coming and going, a fully prepped and organized purse is crucial to managing your time and your life well. Having a special hook for your purse in the entry area makes it super easy to grab and go (no more running late due to searching the house for a wayward pocketbook!).

Tidy up your purse and declutter your wallet to prepare yourself for whatever the day brings—whether that's a business meeting or a class or a volunteer activity. Remember, an organized purse puts you further along the path to an organized life!

1. Clear out your purse completely, including your wallet, emptying all pockets and containers.

2. Recycle wrappers and trash and file away all necessary receipts and papers.

3. Put essential cash, debit or credit cards, and health cards back into your wallet.

4. Add small, zippered pouches to corral loose items for better organization and easier access (makeup, reward cards, coins, and personal items).

5. Designate a particular pocket for your cell phone and keys so you can easily grab them when needed. Slip in a small notebook for jotting down essential notes or shopping needs.

6. Create your own little purse-sized emergency kit so you're prepared for anything. Include a few first aid supplies (such as Band-Aids and pain medication), toiletries, laundry pen, mints, and cash.

You can also use these steps when you're cleaning out tote bags, backpacks, or beach bags that tend to get cluttered and messy. A quick weekly upkeep is all you need!

DIY | COMMAND CENTRAL CABINET

Repurpose a small cabinet or dresser (or even the inside of a kitchen cabinet or linen closet) to create a stylish landing spot for important entryway necessities.

Here's a handy list of tips and ideas to make over your own DIY Command Central cabinet:

+ Adhesive or other shallow hooks can be installed inside a cabinet door to organize extra keys and even a flashlight for power outages.

+ Clip up an easy-to-grab list of emergency phone numbers (or use a magnetic board).

+ Put peel-and-stick cork squares on the inside of a cabinet door for keeping important household notes organized. (Add a note with your Wi-Fi password.)

+ Labeled trays on shelves corral family paperwork or incoming or outgoing mail.

+ Bins can hold gadgets or personal belongings.

+ Add a babysitter or dogsitter notebook with important instructions to leave with anyone caring for your kids or pets.

+ Design an electronic charging station in a drawer or cubby (drill a hole through the back of a cabinet for the cords) to house all those gadgets and battery chargers.

+ Set up a hospitality notebook filled with favorite restaurants and shopping destinations for guests.

7 MAKE A MAIL SORTING STATION

Some of the craziest clutter in the entryway is caused by mail—from bills to junk mail to magazines to important correspondence. It's easy to keep adding to a pile or overflow a basket or tray with paper, which also makes it easy to miss payments or misplace documents.

No matter how much entry space you have, it's easy to designate a drop zone or command center system for organizing paper near the front door.

+ Wire baskets mounted on the walls make a cute and rustic mail station. Consider using several baskets: an "in" basket and an "out" basket, or perhaps a separate basket for each member of the family.

+ An old-fashioned wooden mail sorter provides room for incoming and outgoing mail, stamps, envelopes, note cards (perfect for dashing off quick thank-you letters), and pens.

+ Add file folders to your mail station for increased organization.

+ Use built-in shelves, bookcases, or flat surfaces, such as the top of a piano if you don't have an entry table or separate entry space.

+ Hang a clipboard on the wall for correspondence and bills that need your immediate attention.

+ Buckets or decorative tin pails work well on flat surfaces. You can find fun, colorful patterns and designs.

+ Important school papers and other documents can be included in your mail station. Include any items that tend to get scattered around the house or lost in a desk drawer or backpack.

+ A big basket for mail gives you a start on the organizing process. It's a simple solution to disorganized piles, and you can get more detailed later on if you need to.

Living Spaces

Living Spaces
MAKE YOUR
LIVING AREA LOVABLE

Perhaps no room causes as much organization confusion as the living room. It's often hard to assess our needs in this space. Maybe you've been led to believe that every home needs a formal living room, so you've created just that, but then you find you don't use it. Perhaps this space sits unused, yet the rest of your house doesn't have enough space to accommodate your needs. Or maybe your living room has morphed into a catchall of activity, but it's so chock-full of stuff that nobody can actually relax or accomplish much of anything in there.

Give yourself permission to repurpose this space in a way that works for your family. Make it attractive so you'll be drawn to enjoy it, but practical and sensible enough to be useful for this season of life. A living room doesn't have to be fancy, and it shouldn't be just wasted space. Make this a room you can actually live in.

Set up your living room to be organized and used for what you truly need and love. Feel free to change things up as your needs change. Surround yourself with things that matter now. Decorate with items that put a smile on your face. Organize with fun, communication, and connection in mind. Above all, your living space is for *you*. Make it your own, make it work for you, and make it work for your family.

8 | MAKE MEMORIES

Do you long to gather some friends together to start a book club or other group? Do your kids need a good hangout space for their friends—or do you need hangout space of your own for when friends or neighbors stop by? Do you dream of family fun nights?

When you're organizing your living space, focus on the word *living*. What kind of memories do you want to make? What will bring laughter to your home? What kind of environment will foster long conversations and sharing?

+ If you dream of family game nights around a real board game, stop dreaming and clear out that armoire or those cluttered shelves in your living room and create an organized space for family games. Donate any games you haven't played in forever and keep only your favorites. You can also swap games with friends to determine if you really want to own them (or just keep a lending library going).

+ People stay where they feel comfortable. Cozy couches and chairs need to be cleared of stuff before people will consider making themselves at home. Also, concentrate on eliminating the clutter from coffee tables or end tables. And sometimes a soft rug (again, free of stuff!) is the best place for a casual hangout.

+ Don't feel that you need to have a perfectly picked-up living room. Too pristine can sometimes be as unsettling as too messy. If guests feel uncomfortable sitting in your space, they won't stay long. Scattered books, family photos, a game in progress on an ottoman, fresh flowers from the garden, or some knitting in a basket by the sofa all say, "We live here. We have fun here. We make memories here."

9 | QUESTION EVERYTHING

Look at what has been hanging on the walls of your living room or sitting on a table or in a cabinet for seemingly forever. What is the story of that item? If you rarely use it, or if it doesn't have a good story that means something to you, let it go! Most things can be easily and affordably replaced if you find you truly do need them later. Better to let go and have to replace something than to hang on to an excessive amount of stuff you may never use again. Chances are, the more you keep, the less you use. Let it go and feel your stress go too.

The process of decluttering can be strangely addicting, and it's easy to move on from that point.

Reset your space back to its original state. It may sound a little extreme, but clearing absolutely everything out of your living room might give you a new vision for how to make the most of your valuable space.

Surround yourself with favorite mementos and objects that remind you of family and friends. You don't have to be surrounded by empty surfaces and barren bookshelves. A manageable number of happy things you love will breathe life and soul into your living room. The less you keep, the more you appreciate what really matters.

Resist becoming emotionally attached to too much stuff. Before you bring an item into your living room, ask yourself, *Do I really enjoy it? Is it a charming addition or just additional clutter to dust around? Is it functional? Do I have a distinct place and purpose for it?* When in doubt, it's better to keep less than to try to style, clean, and organize excess.

Imagine yourself as a gallery curator who changes up the collection somewhat frequently when displaying kids' art or even your accessories. Display a rotating collection of art on a doorway or inspiration wire. Or set aside wall space for the latest masterpieces. (The same method works well for photos.) Challenge yourself to keep only a few accessories or rotate in your favorites. Too much will tend to turn to clutter.

Discover a balance of things that works for you as you bring items in and out of your living space. You'll know you've added too much if the room starts to feel overwhelming for *your* personal taste. Less is more when it comes to being organized, so opt for more function and style with less.

10 | IDENTIFY YOUR FAMILY/ PERSONAL STYLE

When you're assessing your living room, it's important to take a good, hard look at where you're at in life. Does the space match your current season? Do you need to add in some kid-friendly items, or do you need to put away things everyone has outgrown? This can be an overwhelming—and sometimes emotional—process, but it's one that always has a positive outcome.

1. After you've done the initial decluttering to remove unnecessary items, look around and see how much more inviting your space is with clear surfaces and uncluttered corners!

2. Do you have unused furniture in this room that might contribute to an overly crowded or cluttered ambience? When a room has too many unnecessary pieces of furniture, there isn't breathing room to relax or enjoy gathering in that space. What could be relocated or rearranged to streamline and update your living room? Take some time to better utilize this space.

3. Things you collect—books, movie tickets, postcards, art from travels, quotes that mean something special to you—can be fun to display. If the items are sentimental and fit your sense of style, by all means show them off. They're terrific conversation starters, plus they make you smile. Get mementos out of storage and turn what you love into meaningful art.

4. Assess the activities that take place—or that you wish would take place—in your living area. Do you need more space for sitting down and having lingering conversations? Or does the floor need to be clear for games and active play? Take a realistic look at the needs of those who live in, as well as frequently visit, your home, and make decisions based on your current reality.

5. Just as there are many different personality types, there are various ways to organize. If a comfortable amount of meaningful clutter makes you happy, embrace it. If you breathe more easily in sparse, clean spaces, love that look. Remember, your living room isn't a showplace. It's a place for you and others to enjoy.

11 | REPURPOSE YOUR SPACE IF NECESSARY

Do you actually *use* a formal living area, or would that room be better repurposed as an alternative space? Depending on the size of your home and the needs of those who occupy it, you might rethink using the space in a way that better suits your family.

Think *purpose*. What is important to you? What are your family's current interests? What do you wish you had more room to do?

Be flexible. Use creativity. You can combine interests to create a unique, one-of-a-kind room where family and friends are certain to gather, relax, and become inspired. How could you better organize the living space you have to make room for valued activities?

Divide your room into activity zones to organize the space for multiple uses, or even repurpose a room for your unique needs.

+ If you love books and art, turn a corner of your space into a library/gallery/art room.

+ Performing families could take advantage of an extra room to have a music and movie area.

+ You could combine a home office with a homeschool area.

Is your space limited or still feeling too cramped for everything you need? Make choices for what can stay and what should be relocated to a different spot. If you play board games more than you read, store the books elsewhere and put the games front and center. Kids constantly begging for read-aloud time? Move out the decorative items and replace them with children's literature. Need space to stretch and unwind? Eliminate an unused chair and create an exercise corner. If you love it, you need to make room for it!

AFTER

BEFORE

12 | SET SOME GOALS

As you're organizing your main living space, have your ideal end result in mind. Set reasonable goals in words and pictures. Put your organizing plan into motion with an eye toward an achievable goal. This will help you stay on track and not become overwhelmed.

ESTABLISH YOUR LIVING ROOM'S PURPOSE

How do you want to use this room? As a place for rejuvenation? A place to unwind with family? A place to welcome new friends? Defining the purposes of your home will help you set appropriate goals for organizing your space.

LOOK FOR NEW IDEAS

Peruse magazines, Pinterest, and blogs for specific organizing ideas that will work for your space. Look for simple solutions to organize your bookshelves, create more open space by rearranging furniture, and display your treasures in a clutter-free, aesthetically pleasing way.

GATHER INSPIRATION PHOTOS

Look at your favorite inspiration room. Notice how much stuff is pictured and compare that to your own room. I know it's tempting to simply dismiss the inspiration room as unachievable perfection when there is not a dirty dish or pile of laundry in sight. As you rethink how you use your space, declutter, and organize your necessities, your home can look just as neat and clutter-free as your favorite inspiration room (after a quick tidying up, of course). What storage pieces are in your inspiration room? How could you creatively incorporate similar functional places for everything you need in your living space?

BE CREATIVE WITH WHAT YOU HAVE

While it may feel overwhelming to look at your growing wish list of organizers or furniture you want for your living room (especially as you surf Pinterest boards!), remember that it's often more cost effective to find creative solutions or use what you have in a different way.

Paint gives new life to just about any piece of furniture. Wallpaper (or giftwrap) on the backs of cabinets or surfaces of boxes can add personality to a humdrum piece. Keep your eye out at thrift shops and yard sales for unique pieces that could be used to streamline or organize your home.

Allow the space to evolve naturally—and enjoy the activity!

13 | MAKE ROOM FOR WHAT YOU LOVE

Homes are most beautiful when they are fully lived in and loved on, don't you think? Let's face it, living rooms will get messy (if we actually live there, that is). The day's homework or projects might be scattered on the coffee table. Kid and dog toys might be all over the floor, signs of a happy and active family. Give yourself grace for the everyday mess that tends to multiply in well-loved spaces.

But if you want to have room for the things you truly love, your space will need to be regularly cleared of the things you are *not* using or currently enjoying. Surfaces covered with last week's dishes and months of unopened junk mail, and floors covered with dirty laundry or clutter, don't allow room for living well today. Remove or put away what is no longer needed in that space, making room for new projects and experiences!

BY WISDOM A HOUSE IS BUILT AND THROUGH UNDERSTANDING IT IS ESTABLISHED; THROUGH KNOWLEDGE ITS ROOMS ARE FILLED WITH RARE AND BEAUTIFUL TREASURES PROVERBS 24:3

Start organizing this space by assessing what types of messes you have in the living room at the end of every day. Papers? Books? Art or hobbies? Electronics? Schoolwork? Dinner dishes? Clothes? Coats? Blankets? Laundry?

Set up a plan to resolve each problem with a practical solution.

+ A closed storage piece can streamline the look of a room while providing a location for craft supplies.

+ A stack of lidded baskets could stash your handcrafts and hobbies so you can bring them out as needed and put them away with ease.

+ Books and magazines look better organized in trays or baskets instead of piled in haphazard stacks.

+ Library books are best kept in their own storage container. Designating a separate basket or shelf for library items makes them easy to locate when they're due. Best way to avoid stress and fines.

+ Remotes and devices can live in their own tray, basket, or wood box too.

+ Cords can be tamed with special cord-keeping devices.

+ Flat surfaces should stay as clutter-free as possible. Resist the urge to fill an empty space. In a room full of activity that can easily become cluttered, margins and breathing room are even more important.

+ Furniture with hidden storage is ideal for media, games, magazines, and hobbies (such as yarn and needles for knitting). Keep your eye out for benches and ottomans that provide extra seating as well as storage.

+ A storage ottoman makes the perfect rotating toy box for little ones. Change up the toy selection by month or season.

+ Current newspapers and magazines can be corralled in a big basket, which is way more organized than pages scattered everywhere.

+ Need more storage space? The best way to create additional storage space is to get rid of what you don't use in that space to make room for what you do use.

14 | STRIKE A HAPPY MEDIUM

What inspires you to be happy at home? What brings you peace? What brings laughter into your living room? Design and organize your home to reflect the personality of your family. Accessories and mementos can bring laughter or joy, but stuff that isn't loved and cared for becomes clutter.

Give yourself small goals. Even if you're tempted, you don't have to get rid of everything or start redecorating from scratch. That might be unrealistic—and expensive! When you eliminate what you don't need or love, the pieces that are keepers really pop. If you have too many accessories, reduce them by 50 percent. If your living room still looks cluttered, go through again and remove another 25 percent. Keep going until you strike the perfect balance and have pared things down to what feels right to you.

Surround yourself with what you love, but not too much! My family happens to love books and decor. But if our storage areas are full of things we love, if we can't find what we are looking for, or if what we have is always dusty and rarely used, we know it's time to let some of what we love go. Send treasures off to be enjoyed by a new family. Letting go can be an unexpected blessing to both of you.

🐦 **Tip:** Make it a family rule to put personal belongings away before bedtime. Look around the room to see what's out of place and do a quick tidy up to put the room back together again for the next day. It's much easier to restore order to a space each evening than it is to let the messes pile up for weeks.

Kitchen & Dining Room

Kitchen & Dining Room

PREPARING FOR COOKING
AND CONNECTION

When your cabinets are sticky and your drawers are full of crumbs, or you can't find room for your everyday necessities because every cabinet and drawer is filled to the brim, working in the kitchen can be a frustrating experience.

The never-ending cycle of meal prepping and cleanup in a kitchen can cause even type A personalities to throw in the towel on cleaning and organization and say, "Forget it! I give up. It's just going to get messy again in a few hours!"

Same with the dining room. Kids do homework there. Parents pay bills. Little ones get going on elaborate craft projects. Often, there's hardly any space left to actually set down plates and glasses for a meal. Piles grow and multiply, and meals are shifted elsewhere or simply eaten on the go.

It may take a bit of time, but you can apply the same simple organizing methods to your kitchen and dining areas. Start by arranging your area into task zones. Take a realistic look at what you need to accomplish and the items you need to do it. Figure out workable solutions for storage. As always, get rid of what you never use to free up space for your necessities. And put an easy-to-implement routine into place.

Once you've taken these simple steps, you'll feel so much more content with your kitchen and family-friendly dining area. These areas are the heart of the home, where you nourish body and soul. They're worth the effort to make them feel as inviting and functional as possible.

15 | POWER CLEAN AND ESTABLISH A ROUTINE

Just a few steps performed on a regular basis help you get your kitchen in shape so you can get on with the fun stuff.

Ready for a power clean? Let's do this.

1. Unload the dishwasher and put away all clean dishes. Load the dishwasher with all dirty dishes. Clean all pots and pans and wash anything that needs to be hand-washed until you have an empty sink.

2. Clean the stovetop.

3. Wipe down appliances, blenders, microwaves, and toaster ovens. Run soapy water through your blender to clean it. Polish up cabinets to clear fingerprints or smudges.

4. Clear and wipe off all counters.

5. Take out the garbage.

6. Sweep the floors and then mop to shine them up.

7. Deep clean your sink. (For my white, cast-iron sink, I use Bon Ami or baking soda and Castile soap to make my own cleaning paste. Check with your sink manufacturer for how to safely clean yours.) Polish the faucet.

8. Enjoy the daily tidying ritual. Invest in pretty dish towels (free up space in a drawer by storing towels in a wire basket by the sink), and set a brand-new dish-scrubbing brush in a pitcher or jar.

Tip: A cleaner home is a healthier home too! Pare down the harsh and harmful chemicals under your sink. Stick to baking soda, vinegar, or a few plant-based products for the health of family and friends. You can add scent and naturally deodorize with pure essential oils. Try basil, lavender, lemon, or geranium to make your kitchen smell like a garden. And with fewer products under the sink, you'll have even more room for other things you need.

16 | ARRANGE AREAS INTO TASK ZONES

Do you ever experience avalanches in your kitchen? Is it hard to find room for dishes or food in your cabinets because they're already filled to the brim? Does preparing meals take forever because it's impossible to find your ingredients?

No matter what size kitchen you have, it's helpful to arrange the space according to the tasks you need to perform in it. Don't worry about perfection here. While drawer dividers and labels can be attractive and handy, it's best to start simply. Silverware or gadgets tossed in drawers works just fine—as long as they're the correct drawers. When everything is within easy access, kitchen work is just more efficient!

Figure out what zones your kitchen might need and how small areas might be best utilized.

- A baking zone (muffin tins and baking dishes, utensils, mixing bowls)

- A cooking zone (pots and pans with lids, casserole/baking dishes, serving dishes and bowls, colanders and strainers, cooking utensils, herbs and spices, cooking oils)

- A food storage zone (glass or plastic storage containers, labeling supplies)

- An everyday dishes zone (dinner plates, saucers, cups, bowls)

- A coffee or tea zone (coffee, tea bags, mugs, stirrers, flavored syrups, sweeteners)

- A chopping zone (cutting boards, knives, vegetable peeler, other gadgets)

- A cleanup zone (hand soap, dish soap, dishwasher detergent, scrubber, dish towels, dish drainer, compost and recycling containers)

17 | DEAL WITH THE DISHES

While clean dishes make me smile, dirty dishes make me downright cranky. And a sink filled with dirty, smelly dishes makes it easy to say, "Forget cooking dinner tonight! Let's go out." (Maybe three nights in a row?) The main mess in a kitchen usually involves a pileup of dirty dishes. So what can we do? We can deal with them—right now!

Load the dishwasher and run it at night. Do it every night. Even when you're tired. Waking up to a counter piled with dirty dishes is guaranteed to start the day with additional stress and will lead to even more clutter and pileups. Be sure to collect dishes from every room in the house before you run the dishwasher to keep other areas clean too.

Unload the dishwasher every morning. This makes it easy to load dishes in throughout the day while keeping your sink and counter space clear.

Sort silverware before you wash it. This makes unloading the dishwasher a breeze.

Don't stack dirty dishes in the sink. Make it a policy to load them into the dishwasher right away or wash them by hand. The exception: You can soak the super dirty stuff or stack dishes in a bin to keep the sink clear while you're cooking. But tackle those dishes ASAP too!

Wash and rinse as you go. As you cook and bake, do the dishes. When you're waiting for water to boil, wash and dry a few mixing bowls. Reuse dishes and utensils as you go for less mess and easier cleanup at the end.

Open shelving works well for quick cleanup. If you're short on cabinet space, free up additional room with open shelving for everyday plates and bowls. Dishes are easy to put away when you can just place them on open shelves. I like an all-white dish theme for open shelves. Even if the pieces don't match, the white gives a simple, clean, and coordinated look.

Motivate yourself. Make the most of time spent doing dishes. Light a favorite candle. Listen to music or a podcast. Reward yourself with a little treat when your kitchen chores are completed.

18 | FIGURE OUT FOOD STORAGE AND ORGANIZATION

+ Create zones for organizing your stored food: snacks, breakfast items, pastas, sauces, bulk foods, canned goods, soups, etc.

+ Collect baskets, wire or metal bins, and colorful crates or metal buckets over time for cupboard and pantry storage. Cute and functional, these keep you organized while adding a bit of decorative pop.

+ It's impossible to organize clutter. Bite the bullet and toss any food that is expired or that you know your family won't eat.

+ Store bulk items, such as grains, beans, and oatmeal, in large glass jars. Buy in bulk to save money and store what's not in the jars in bags hidden inside decorative crates, buckets, or baskets. Simply refill your jars as needed.

+ Use chalkboard labels to identify anything that's not easily visible. These look adorable affixed to baskets, crates, or other containers. If it's labeled, it's likely to be used.

+ Store paper plates, plastic utensils, and other seldom-used items in baskets up and away from the things you grab on a more frequent basis.

+ Make sure snacks are easily visible in a wire crate or basket. This ensures they'll be eaten before they become stale. Keep things tidy and save money at the same time.

+ Put small, preprepared containers in the fridge to organize cold lunch items, snacks, drinks, veggies, and fruit to take to school or work.

+ Your goal should be the least complicated system that works for you. Everyone organizes on different levels. Go with what works for your household and stick to your system!

19 CREATE MORE SPACE IN YOUR KITCHEN

No matter the size of our kitchens, they always seem to be a little short on space. And no longer are they equipped with just a few appliances, such as a dishwasher, stove, and oven. Add to the mix microwaves, blenders, stand mixers, food processors, coffeemakers, rice cookers, food dehydrators...all designed to make our life simpler, but each one takes up valuable space in our cabinets! That's where paring down to necessities and making the most of your storage makes sense. You might not be able to add square footage or counter space, but you *can* be smart with the space you have.

+ Assess what small appliances you use on a regular basis. You may be able to streamline a few to one appliance that is more multifunctional. You'll likely discover that you really don't use all of your small appliances, so pare down to only the gadgets you can't live without.

+ Add a wall-mounted magnetic knife holder to free up drawer or counter space.

+ Save cupboard space by adding a hanging pot rack or hooks on the wall for frequently used pots.

+ Use stackable nesting bowls and measuring cups to best utilize drawer or cupboard areas. Items that don't nest take up excess space.

+ Add a rolling island or kitchen cart with a drop-leaf surface to expand counter space. Attach hooks or a towel rod to the side for additional storage.

+ Utilize the backs of cupboards by adding over-the-cupboard organizers, painting them with chalkboard paint for grocery lists, or posting a corkboard to pin recipes. Attach magnetic boards and magnetized spice holders to cabinet doors.

+ Hang open shelves in the kitchen or pantry to make the most of your kitchen's available vertical spaces.

+ Organize the area below the sink for better efficiency. Add hooks, rolling storage drawers, risers, bins, or even a lazy Susan to maximize the space. Try a tension rod to hang cleaning bottles or a towel bar for garbage bags.

+ Place a crock by the stove to hold your most-used kitchen utensils to free up drawer space.

+ Add baskets in the empty spaces above your cabinets to keep items you use less often, such as turkey pans and holiday-themed cookie cutters.

+ Add a hanging wall file organizer with slots to the inside of your cabinet to hold pan lids.

+ Add a lazy Susan for canned goods and spices.

+ Put risers inside the kitchen cabinets as needed to optimize space.

DIY | UNDER THE KITCHEN SINK

The space under your sink is often underutilized or overstuffed. Take some time to transform that valuable real estate into a space with purpose and function. Here are six simple steps to reorganize the space under your sink:

1. Clear out everything so you start with an empty cabinet.

2. Wipe down and clean out the space.

3. Assess what products or items need to be kept under the sink.

4. Set up a drawer system or add risers in the cabinet to add additional storage.

5. Adhere self-adhesive hooks and containers to vertical surfaces (such as the cabinet doors) to conveniently corral small items, such as brushes and sponges.

6. Use containers (baskets or pails work great!) to organize supplies, such as garbage bags, towels, or other necessities. If you have room, add a lazy Susan for spray bottles and cleaning supplies.

20 | DELIGHT IN YOUR DINING AREA

Flat surfaces are where we tend to dump and pile, and the largest flat surface in your home is most likely your dining room table. Quick—take a peek and see what's currently residing there. Homework? Dirty dishes? Stacks of mail? Toys or packages? Laundry? It's easy to use your dining room as a storage area for a random assortment of things, but you can also decide to make it a place to nurture people and create memorable experiences.

1. Does all the clutter on your dining room table actually belong somewhere else in the house? Gather it all up in a big basket and return the items to their rightful places. Declare your dining table a clutter-free zone! Anything that is brought to the table should be taken away when the activity is completed or by mealtime.

2. See your table as a sacred family gathering space where you offer nourishment to those you love. Clearing the clutter, wiping down the table, and sweeping the floor as you prepare the table for the next meal can become a soothing ritual every day rather than an ongoing annoyance.

3. A buffet, shelves, or other furniture in the dining room doesn't have to be only for dishes. It can hold anything you regularly use at the table, such as coloring books and crayons, a radio, books and projects, art supplies, a container of pens and pencils for doing homework, or a bill-paying basket.

4. Keep something nice on the table at all times, such as a mason jar of fresh flowers or a pretty tablecloth to discourage clutter.

5. Gather items that you can bring out when you want to set up a special meal for family and when entertaining friends. Find cloth napkins in fun patterns or make them out of fabric. Include a set of pretty drinking glasses. Collect dessert or salad plates to dress up your everyday dishes. Gather unscented, colored candles and unique candlesticks (don't forget birthday candles!). Have these items well organized and easily accessible in a basket, dresser, or small cabinet for a spontaneous special meal.

21 | SIMPLIFY MEALTIMES

Do you find yourself running to the grocery store five times a week (sometimes it feels like five times a day)? Are you constantly wondering what to make for dinner? Do you have a fridge full of food but nothing to eat? After you've organized your kitchen, it's time to organize your meal planning.

+ Make a list of five go-to meals that your family loves and are easy to prepare in a hurry. Post your standard meal list inside a cupboard. Next, write out a list of pantry items and fresh food needed to make those meals and keep a copy in your wallet or with your shopping list. Take a photo of the list if it's easier to locate on the go. Each week, assess what you have from the list and replenish when you go shopping so you always have at least five meal options on hand for nights when you are too tired or busy to make something new.

+ Always, always try to plan ahead. At first it may seem like more work, but planning always saves you time in the end.

+ Plan to grocery shop just once a week instead of giving it your first thought at six p.m. and then running out feeling frazzled as you try to decide what to prepare. If you chop and prep the week's veggies on Sunday afternoon, you'll save time later as well as eat more vegetables and less junk.

+ Prep and plan breakfasts and lunches the day before. You can create hundreds of versions of overnight oatmeal, and sandwiches and protein-filled salads make great go-to lunches. Thinking one step ahead will save you stress and frustration the following morning.

Master Bedroom

Master Bedroom

REORDER AND REFRESH
YOUR RELAXATION SPACE

The master bedroom is often the last room we consider organizing because it's usually not on display for others to see. We can close the door when guests arrive, and nobody will think any less of us. (And let's be real. Sometimes we keep the door closed because, in our mad dash to tidy up, we toss all the extra stuff in the master bedroom!)

It's time to rethink this. We spend a lot of time in a bedroom. Never mind that the majority of that time is spent sleeping. Actually, scratch that. *Consider* that the majority of that time is spent sleeping—and that a good night's sleep is the key to an energy-filled, productive day. The last thing you need to feel before crawling into bed is chaos and tension.

Your bedroom should be a relaxing, restful retreat. A few moments spent sipping a cup of chamomile tea and reading a few pages of a book before you turn out the lights work wonders for calming your mind and preparing your body to rejuvenate. Even if you have a crazy-busy day ahead of you, jam-packed with meetings and deadlines and activities and appointments, your bedroom disorganization doesn't have to contribute to the stress of the day.

From paring down the items on the bedside table to editing your wardrobe, in this section you'll gain simple organizing tools to bring calm and relaxation into your bedroom—and into your life.

22 DISCOVER THE DOMINO EFFECT

There's this thing called the *domino effect*. Once you take the first step (or knock down the first domino), it becomes easier and more motivating to do the next thing, especially as you see the rewards of your efforts. This is true for work and exercise and personal growth. It's also true for cleaning and organizing!

Once you begin to tidy your bedroom, you'll want to keep the momentum going. Not sure where to start? Choose one of these tasks and continue on...and on...and on.

+ Remove as many items from the room as you can to create a peaceful space.

+ Make your bed in the morning. (You'll be glad you took the time.)

+ Wash sheets, pillowcases, and blankets on a regular basis.

+ Clear off nightstands and tidy them up.

+ Remove clutter from floors.

+ Vacuum carpet or rugs, or sweep and dust hardwood floors.

+ Clean out under the bed.

+ Dust all surfaces, baseboards, lampshades, and window sills.

+ Polish up accessories and lamps.

+ Put away clean laundry.

+ Fluff and line up pillows.

23 | ELIMINATE EXCESS TO MAKE ROOM FOR STYLE

Remember when we talked about stepping in your front entry and seeing it in a new way? Try to do that with the other rooms in your home, such as the master bedroom.

Make your bedroom a peaceful destination. It's worth the decluttering and the extra organizing because you spend so much of your life in this room. Make it a priority for this space to be as orderly and refreshing as possible so you'll look forward to spending time there dressing, relaxing, and dreaming.

Add hooks to the back of your doors. Make it simple to hang a towel, robe, purse, or even your outfit for the day to keep everything off the floor or bed.

Place an attractive laundry hamper in the space where you get dressed.

Add a plant to purify the air and bring natural, clutter-free decor to the space.

Gather all your accessories (scarves, jewelry, bags) and choose what you actually use. Donate or give away what you don't wear anymore, and then hang the rest on hooks or store in beautiful containers. Make your accessories feel like pieces of art in your bedroom or closet. Set up a simple system and a home for each type of accessory.

Simplify your jewelry organizing. No need to go shopping right away for fancy organizers. Necklaces can be hung on the wall with hooks or on a pretty bulletin board with pushpins. Hang earrings from a ribbon on a wall or on a corkboard. Bracelets can find a home on a plate or trinket dish, on hooks, or in a shallow basket.

Pare down your stuff to keep your organizing system simple. You need plenty of space to breathe in the bedroom.

24 | WHIP YOUR WARDROBE INTO SHAPE

Overwhelmed by choices? Offer yourself fewer options in what you wear or keep in your closet, and it will be easier to decide what to wear and quickly get ready for your day. You'll also do less laundry. And you'll have less to buy to coordinate with all the random items you never wear because you no longer keep those random things you don't wear. Less clothing results in a more orderly closet, so tidying up will be a breeze.

Avoid temptation. Limit window shopping (in stores or online) as it will cause you to buy more clothes, shoes, or accessories to deal with or tempt you with more decisions that will need to be made. It's amazing how much less you buy and how much easier your subsequent decisions are when you spend less time shopping.

When in doubt, throw it out. When you're paring down your wardrobe, you don't have time to analyze every possible item. If you haven't worn something in the past year, you probably won't wear it again. Don't think about how much money you spent on it. Donate the item to a worthy cause or a good friend and move on.

Do you already have the item in the same or a different color? Is life better with two nearly identical clothing items, or can you make do with just one?

Choose three items you could easily remove from your closet. These may be items that don't fit well or aren't really your style or color. Put them in a giveaway bag for someone who will feel beautiful in them. If you're feeling inspired, choose three more items...and three more...and three more.

Still feeling indecisive about an item? Choose to let that thing go. If you ever find a new one that you really love and know you'll use, you can replace it. But chances are, you probably won't miss it.

25 | REMEMBER YOUR ROUTINE

The best way to get your day off to a good start is with a simple morning routine that doesn't take too much work yet makes you feel happy and productive from the start.

+ Disorder in the morning is a domino that causes even more disorder by the evening. Simple routines help you wake up energized and ready to tackle the day. You know what you need to do...and you start doing those things automatically once they've become a habit.

+ Let your bed-making ritual be an enjoyable part of your morning. Spritz a linen spray or essential oil blend on your sheets before you pull up the covers. Find special pillows to prop up against your headboard and a beautiful throw to drape across the end of the bed. (If you have pets or kids, find one that is machine washable.)

+ Making your bed and straightening up your bedroom before you leave for the day allow you to return to an orderly, calm space that evening. Even if the best you can do is to quickly straighten out the sheets and blanket and prop up your pillows before you leave the room, you'll feel less frazzled when you return. A peaceful evening is worth a few extra moments at the start of the day.

+ It's important to incorporate enjoyable little rituals into your morning. I have a coffee station all set up with my favorite mugs, a milk foamer, and a French press so I can mindlessly but mindfully indulge in my morning coffee. I might sit for a few moments in silence, relaxing and enjoying the view outside our window. This little ritual is often the nudge that gets me up and out of bed!

+ A few simple habits establish a rhythm of order in a day. My morning routine, which involves quiet time, making my bed, taking a shower, and getting dressed (right down to my makeup, shoes, and even earrings) sets the rest of my day in a positive direction.

+ Morning habits bring more clarity and peace to every day because they are decisions you don't have to make. They are tasks that have already been decided. You just have to follow through.

26 | PUT YOUR CLOSETS AND DRAWERS TO WORK

The first step in the simple organizing of closets and drawers is getting rid of what you don't need. Once you have what works for you, make smart use of your storage space.

+ Develop an eye for order. When you see untidy closets and drawers, take a few moments to group like items and straighten wayward pieces.

+ Picture the organizing style of your favorite boutique clothing shop. The items are folded neatly on the shelves. Everything is within reach, and nothing is stacked too high. You're able to select clothes with ease because they are hung with breathing room between them on attractive matching hangers.

+ Organize your closet (and make getting ready to head out the door easier) by grouping like items. Shirts together, pants together, dresses together. While you can organize by color if that inspires you, items will look especially tidy if each category is grouped by the length of the item.

+ Make a visual note of how much space you have for your hanging items. Choose to only hang in-season clothes you actually wear regularly and are in good condition.

+ If your closet is still stuffed even after paring down items, see if anything currently hanging up could be folded (such as jeans or T-shirts) and stored elsewhere. Likewise, if your drawers are crammed but your closet has extra space, hang up some items.

+ Invest in matching hangers! Count how many hangers you need and only buy that amount. Your closet will look tidier if the hangers are the same style or at least the same color. Buy slim, nonslip hangers whenever possible.

+ Make the shelves in your closet functional (decide how many items you can stack without it being a hassle to get them out) and fold the items carefully so they look tidy. Group purses, shoes, sweaters, and T-shirts.

+ Shoes can be tucked into back-of-the-door or wall shoe pockets, an extra drawer, or an under-the-bed organizer for easy access if you don't have room in your closet. Make a list of organizers or supplies you'll eventually need to make the most of the space you have.

27 | CREATE A COZY NEST

The mood of your sanctuary can be transformed by daily choices. Streamline your bedroom so it feels both calm and cozy. As you declutter, organize, and decorate, make deliberate choices that will inspire you to rest and take comfort in your space. Say yes to what brings order and peace and no to what increases clutter and stress.

TEXTURES OVER TCHOTCHKES

The bedroom should be a place of rest. Move collections and excess decorations. They just collect dust and are visually distracting. Instead, fill your room with touchable textures. Cozy bedding, rugs, and window treatments quiet a room and elevate the sense of comfort.

MINIMALISM OVER MAXIMALISM

Even if you are naturally more of a maximalist when it comes to design preferences, your bedroom might serve you better if you err on the side of minimalism. Excessive furniture, patterns, and belongings may interfere with the mood you need to sleep or retreat from the hectic pace of life. Where could you streamline and simplify your design?

CURATED OVER CHAOTIC

Look at each element in the room as an opportunity to curate a work of art that inspires you. Look at your walls, your furniture, your fabrics. Select each item to enhance the beauty and peacefulness of the overall space.

CLOSED CABINETS OVER OPEN DISPLAY

Even if your intention is to have a tidy bedroom, nightstand tables with open shelving below can be difficult to maintain. Ideally, closets should have doors or curtains to conceal elements inside. If you must have a computer or office in your bedroom, hide reminders of work in drawers or cabinets.

SERENITY OVER STRESS

Guard your bedroom from unnecessary stress by making this space your sanctuary. Make your bed every day and deal with the laundry elsewhere. Perhaps head to the living room to watch the news and instead play soft music when you retreat to the bedroom. Keep the lights low in the evenings to create a calm, peaceful mood.

28 | DECLUTTER YOUR DRESSER AND BEDSIDE TABLE

Your bedroom might not have many flat surfaces, but the top of the dresser and the bedside table tend to gather stuff—from electronic gadgets to spare change to random receipts. These clutter piles grow and grow until your bedroom becomes a catchall for junk.

Look at your nightstand. What's on it? Dust the surface and only put back what you actually need—perhaps a lamp, a clock or a charger for your cell phone, and a few favorite books neatly stacked and topped with a decorative candle.

Find cute trays and containers to help create order. You can store chargers, jewelry pieces, or even spare change in these while maintaining order on the flat surfaces.

Clean out the drawers in your dresser and bedside tables. Create space for things that are getting piled on top. If you have a nightstand with an open shelf below, stack a nice grouping of books or add a basket that fills the space. That will reduce the temptation to clutter it up!

Add a vase of fresh flowers to the top of the dresser or nightstand. Every time you change the flowers, take the opportunity to dust, declutter, and clean the rest of the surface.

29 | SIMPLIFY WITH ORGANIC STYLE

Decorating with natural elements makes simple organizing easy. You don't have to store or clean the decorations. At the end of the season—or when they've wilted or faded—into the compost bin or yard debris container they go. Good for you, good for the environment.

SPRING

Daffodils, tulips, and iris

Blue glass vases and mason jars

Blooming branches

Moss and twigs

Wildflower bouquets

SUMMER

Shells in a container of sand

River rocks

Blossoms floated in glass bowls

Bouquets of herbs, such as rosemary and lavender

AUTUMN

Mini pumpkins

Asters, chrysanthemums, and sunflowers

Pinecones and sprigs of evergreen

Leaves and branches

WINTER

Pinecones and mini trees

Branches spray-painted gold

Twigs spray-painted white

Baby's breath and evergreen clippings

Bathrooms

Bathrooms

CREATE A SIMPLE
SPA AMBIENCE

While classy bathrooms with marble counters, gorgeous faucets, and beautiful tile make my heart beat a little faster, above all else, clean, uncluttered bathrooms are my favorite. A bathroom sparkling and stocked with fresh towels, toilet paper, soap, and other essentials can almost seem like a brand-new place.

A well-organized bathroom helps you streamline your morning routine. When the bathroom is put together, you feel more put together. Having hair-care items, makeup, and bath supplies simply but attractively ordered and displayed will save you time and sanity. Think pretty yet functional when it comes to storage. Clean and spare. Consider the function of the space—getting yourself ready to go.

The bathroom is a great place to make a shift toward a more natural and healthy lifestyle. Pare down excess and incorporate better quality cleaning and personal products that are good for your body and will make your bathroom feel more luxurious.

And while function is important, don't forget to add a little spa ambience to the bathroom. Sometimes you just need a bubble bath session—or a long, hot shower. Tidy and fresh bathrooms boasting a little charm are a winning combination.

30 | STREAMLINE YOUR CLEANING ROUTINE

Okay, deep breath. Are you ready to give your bathroom a thorough cleaning? You really only have to do this once in a while, and then in between you just maintain. If your bathroom is pretty nasty (and there's no shame in admitting this; it happens to the best—and busiest—of us), don't feel guilty hiring a professional housekeeper to do the job for you. Post this list inside a bathroom cupboard to help you to focus on efficiency.

1. Wash the shower curtain, liner, and any window curtains and blinds.

2. Clean the toilet bowl and polish the top, sides, and toilet base.

3. Scrub the tub or shower.

4. Clean out the medicine cabinet and safely discard old products.

5. Wipe out the drawers.

6. Take out the trash.

7. Rehang the curtains and shower curtain and liner.

8. Clean the mirrors.

9. Polish the counter and sinks and counter accessories.

10. Sweep the floor and mop.

After you've accomplished the big chores, you can maintain the order in five- to ten-minute cleaning bursts. You can start by polishing up the sink in under a minute! Eventually, bathroom cleaning will become second nature, and you'll have a streamlined routine permanently in place.

31

TRANSFORM THE TOWEL AND TOILETRY SUPPLIES

It's easy for our bathrooms to become overrun with towels and toiletries. It may seem impossible to have 80 million products in the shower and no conditioner, but it happens. And all those towels on the floors and counters—which ones are clean or could have been used again?

+ Pare down your towel stash to only the best of the best (perhaps to simplify, set a goal of just two bath towels per person, two hand towels, and several washcloths). Make a note to invest in a new set if your towels look as if they've seen better days.

+ I like using an all-white color scheme for my towel collection. They always match, and a little bleach keeps them looking fresh. This is also a great way to avoid those bleached-out spots that facial cleansers leave on colored towels.

+ Install extra rods and hooks on the back of the door to maximize your space for hanging and drying towels. It's easier to avoid the temptation of throwing your towel on the floor when it's just as easy to hang it up on a designated hook.

+ Keep track of your towels. Sew on simple colored tabs or ribbons to distinguish whose towel is whose. You can also purchase decorative numbered hooks or stencil numbers above hooks and assign a number to each family member. Bonus: Hanging up the towels helps them dry quickly!

+ Store extra supplies (toilet paper, soap, shampoo, and conditioner) in another location but keep track of what you need to repurchase as you run out. It saves money to buy in bulk, and fewer trips to the store also saves significant time.

+ Do you really need to display decorative items on your bathroom counters and shelves? Attractive containers for items you actually use are decoration enough. A basket filled with colorful bath bombs or a mirrored tray holding a few favorite lotions will give the bathroom that simple spa vibe.

32 | CORRAL SUPPLIES IN CREATIVE CONTAINERS

While it might be tempting to go with a specific decorating theme for your bathroom and shop for various items, the reality is that bathrooms easily become cluttered with extra stuff. Attractive containers for items you actually *use* can serve as decor without the added clutter.

1. Hang a small tray, basket, or shelf near the toilet to hold extra toilet paper, a candle, or a natural air freshener spray.

2. Store such necessities as cotton swabs and cotton balls in a fancy jar. That will add a luxurious touch to simple, everyday items. Bonus: Search for free printable container labels if your jars aren't clear.

3. Paint small wooden crates and use screws to mount them on the walls.

4. Fill a lazy Susan with unique containers that hold items from toothbrushes to sunscreen to hair ties.

5. Use uniform plastic bottles for shower essentials such as shampoo, conditioner, and body wash. Besides looking classy, matching containers also fit better on shower shelves or in a wire shower caddy.

6. Mount hooks on out-of-the-way wall space for hair tools, such as curling irons and straighteners. You can also store these in a metal bin or filing box, which makes it safe to put them away while they're still hot.

7. Set perfume or pretty lotion bottles on a mirrored tray. They will decorate your bathroom and be easily accessible.

8. Stand makeup brushes in a jar for easy access.

9. If you have double sinks with space in between on the counter and need more storage space, add a cute basket to stash your hairbrushes or cosmetics, jars for makeup brushes, attractive bottles for bubble bath, or a tiered shelving unit to hold towels or extra supplies. Group similar items into cute containers, baskets, or jars.

10. Use attractive organizers and dividers to keep makeup, accessories, and toiletries orderly in your drawers. Keep counters clear. Your daily items can be just as accessible out of sight in drawers.

33 | CONSIDER SIMPLIFYING YOUR CLEANING PRODUCTS

Have you taken a good look at your favorite cleaning products lately? A while ago, I did an assessment of the items in my cleaning caddy and realized that many of them were laden with harmful chemicals. Because I wanted to eliminate toxins from my home, I replaced them with options that were healthier for my family and healthier for the environment. The process was actually quite painless. Bonus: I ended up with fewer products to organize and store!

Be diligent about reading labels, but don't freak out. Changing up things can actually simplify your cleaning. Remember the natural-living rule of thumb: It's only truly clean if the products you use are healthy and safe.

Question what you use. Many cleaning products contain toxic chemicals. Research ingredients online or in books to see how "natural" a product is. Also, be careful of some candles and air freshener sprays. Healthier alternatives can be found. (A word of advice: Even products labeled "natural" aren't necessarily good for you.)

Embrace essential oils. Use an essential-oil based diffuser, reeds in a glass bottle, a few drops of essential oil on a cotton ball to make your bathroom smell scrumptious or you can make your own spray bottle room freshener. Just be sure you're using pure essential oils with no artificial ingredients added.

Use lemon juice and baking soda to clean your sink. Simple, effective, and totally nontoxic.

Clean out your drains naturally. Pour one-half cup baking soda down the drain, followed by one-half cup vinegar. After it fizzes, pour six cups hot water down the drain.

Clean your toilet bowls quickly and easily. All you need is one-quarter cup baking soda and one cup vinegar. No need for specialty cleaners.

Pare down cleaning products to just one or two all-purpose cleaners. Combine one-half cup vinegar and one-quarter cup baking soda with one-half gallon water. Spot test on sensitive materials, such as countertops or flooring. Add your favorite essential oil to personalize it!

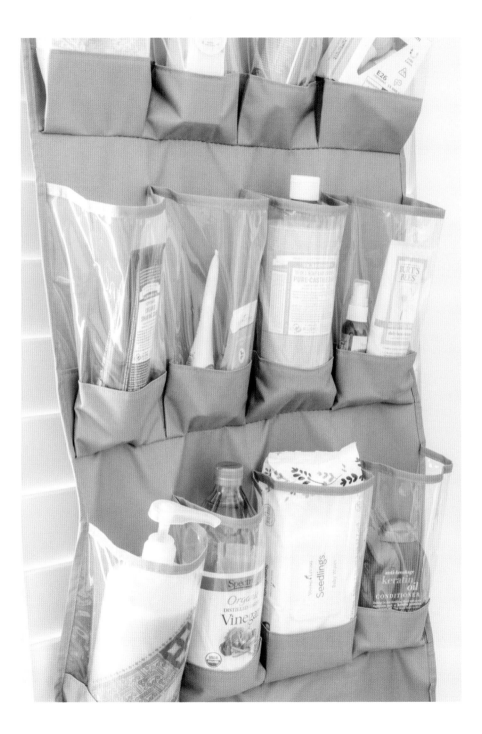

34 | PAMPER WITH A PERSONAL SPA

One of the most productive ways I've found to motivate myself to clean, pare down, and organize a bathroom is to visualize it as though it is my own personal spa.

A day of pampering wouldn't be nearly as inviting if the sinks and counters were covered in soap scum and dried toothpaste. I know I couldn't relax in a spa if it was filled with dirty laundry, trash, or half-empty cosmetic containers.

A bathroom is a destination in your home that deserves a little more care and attention to detail because YOU deserve it. When a bathroom is clean and streamlined, it simplifies daily routines and enhances the whole experience too.

As long as you're committed to the hard work of cleaning and organizing your bathroom, take the opportunity to invest in a few pampering indulgences. Spa accessories can be a positive motivator and a reward for your cleaning efforts.

Invest in spa-like luxuries such as:

+ A long-handled brush for washing your back

+ A hand massager for your neck

+ A luxurious soap or liquid gel

+ A beautiful, fluffy set of clean towels

+ Delicious-smelling soaps. You can even match the scents with the seasons. Lilac and lavender in the spring and summer. Cinnamon and peppermint in the autumn and winter.

If you have the space, place a small stack of your favorite magazines or mystery novels in a basket near the bathtub along with an attractive container of bubble bath to invite yourself to kick back and relax.

Gather a box or drawer of items to pamper guests too, such as a bar soap and body wash, toothbrush and toothpaste, dental floss, shampoo and conditioner, disposable razor and shaving cream, bath towels as well as hand towels and washcloths, a few basic first aid supplies, feminine products, and deodorant.

35 | PARE DOWN BEAUTY PRODUCTS

Products accumulate quickly in the bathroom, but we often reach for just a few favorites. Extra products clutter our space and make us feel disorganized. Take some time to assess what you have and what you actually use.

1. Empty the drawers or any storage containers in the bathroom. Throw away any facial products you don't use or that have expired. Get rid of old or never-used nail polish too.

2. Set aside makeup items you don't use regularly but you think you will be likely to use on special occasions (fancy lipstick or eye shadow, for instance). Put those items in a separate pouch or box that can be placed in a less convenient or visible location. If you find you never end up opening that container, let those items go to make more room for what you actually use.

3. Pare down hair accessories, styling tools, and products to only what you use and love. Look in the shower or tub area and declutter any excess.

4. Group together styling and pampering items by category (hair, face, nails, body, teeth). Gather appropriate containers and organizers. Use what you have to get started. Look around the house for small boxes, saucers, pouches, cosmetic bags, or small bowls. (You can always fancy things up later.) Set up an area, drawer, or basket for each category so everything you need regularly has a home that is convenient and tidy.

36 | LIVE WITH LAUNDRY

Did you know that the average family spends five to seven hours per week in the laundry room? Add to that time spent searching for clean clothes and putting away laundry—that's a lot of time! And a lot of reason to streamline your laundry routine and get organized.

Your home might be blessed with a separate laundry room, but don't worry if your washer and dryer are in your kitchen or another nearby space. Close proximity makes multitasking easy. Fold a load of laundry while you're waiting for water to boil. No matter where it's located, focus on keeping your laundry area clean, tidy, simple, and streamlined.

+ Because laundry is a never-ending chore, make a habit to keep up with it every day. Just doing a load or two a day beats spending all Saturday at the washer and dryer. Save your weekends for something fun!

+ If you need a little more organization, break down your laundry tasks into a more specific daily schedule. Here's an example:

MONDAY	towels and whites
TUESDAY	darks and jeans
WEDNESDAY	delicates, shower curtains, and bath rugs
THURSDAY	family's sheets
FRIDAY	master bedroom sheets and towels

+ Complete the entire task: wash, dry, fold or hang, and put away. Don't add extra steps, such as piling clothes first on the sofa and then putting the clothes in the laundry baskets, where they sit for a day or two before finally making it to the appropriate room, or tossing them on the floor to fold later and then having to rewash because they've been on the floor all week.

+ Keep extra supplies of detergent available so you don't run out (which can slow down your efficiency!).

+ Hang a rod you can use as a drying rack or a place to put clothes to avoid wrinkles as you pull them out of the dryer. You may never need an ironing pile again! Take clothes on hangers straight to closets.

+ Refresh your laundry space. Polish up the washer and dryer and toss out lint. Recycle old detergent containers and put detergent in prettier containers or set them up in an attractive way. A pretty and organized space is so much more inspiring.

+ Hang shoe pockets for preventing clutter in a laundry room. Use them to sort your cleaning rags, trash bags, small vacuum cleaner attachments, and refills for your mop. Fill them with spray bottles (such as stain removers) or use them to hold those stray socks until their mate is found.

+ Sort laundry into three baskets for efficiency (whites, colors, delicates). With a big family, it can be convenient to assign a weekly laundry day for each person's clothing to save time sorting (or to teach children to do their laundry!).

+ Put attractive storage baskets on top of a front loading washer and dryer. (For instance, I have one for delicate/special care items.) Woven baskets can look cute and help prevent piles on the floor. A slender cart might slide next to the washer or dryer for detergents. A wall organizer can make the most of wall space. Make the most of the space you have!

37 | SET UP A WELLNESS STATION

When someone in the household gets a bee sting or a sunburn or a splinter, there's often a mad scramble to find the supplies you need for soothing the situation. Why not organize a wellness station? All you need is a big-enough basket and an assortment of your go-to remedies. You might want to add a first aid book and emergency numbers too. (Special note: If you have young children, please be mindful of keeping certain medications stored out of their reach.)

WELLNESS SUPPLIES

Adhesive tape	Homeopathic medications
Aloe vera gel or lotion	Hot water bottle
Antibiotic ointment	Hydrogen peroxide
Apple cider vinegar	Insect repellant
Arnica gel or cream	Isopropyl alcohol
Bandages	Nail clippers
Bee sting remedies	Nail file
Calendula salve	Scissors
Chapstick	Sunscreen
Coconut oil	Tea tree oil
Epsom salts	Thermometer
Essential oils	Tweezers for splinters
Gauze	Witch hazel
Heating pad	

Kids' Rooms

Kids' Rooms

KEEP UP WITH YOUR
GROWING TRIBE

If you have kids, your home is going to have what we like to call a "lived-in" look. And the younger your kids are (and the more kids you have), the more this statement is going to be true. But lived-in doesn't have to mean dirty or messy or completely disorganized. A home with kids can still be a comfortable, welcoming, and cozy place for everyone to enjoy.

Simple organizing isn't just good for you and your home. It's also good for your kids! When you give children the opportunity to appreciate or make do with what they have, you teach them contentment. When you encourage them to sort through their items and choose things to give away, you encourage them to develop a spirit of sharing. When you offer fewer options for clothing and toys, you offer greater freedom to make quick decisions and move on to the things that truly matter.

Like adults, kids can become overwhelmed with excessive choices and belongings. When my kids were still small, I would sometimes offer them one of two choices (both good options). The limitations gave them the opportunity to still have a say in a matter without overwhelming them.

From a very young age, kids can learn orderly habits and develop lifelong skills in keeping their things clean and organized. As they grow, so do their responsibilities. As parents, we can guide this growth and together master the art of simplicity.

38 | HELP ESTABLISH ORDERLY HABITS

It's important to teach our children to live responsibly and to be satisfied with what they have rather than always wanting more, better, and newer things. When you help kids establish orderly habits, you help build lifelong skills for staying organized. But beyond that, you teach them to realize the value of caring for and being grateful for what they do have.

+ Keep the basic shell of the room tasteful, neutral, and timeless. Kids' tastes and favorites seem to change all the time. One minute your daughter may be all about Rapunzel from *Tangled*, and the next she is obsessed with Elsa from *Frozen*. Constantly changing the whole room with the latest trend would be expensive and time-consuming and would set up a spirit of discontentment with what she has. Keeping the shell of the room basic and timeless makes it easy to do minor updates and transform the space as your child's tastes evolve. You can add in plenty of your child's personality or favorites with elements, such as artwork in frames, pillowcases, colors, etc.

+ Kids' rooms don't need a lot of decoration. Children already have many colorful and interesting things they love to play with or display. Adding elaborate decor pieces can make a room feel visually cluttered. Give children space to show off their artwork and school projects.

+ Children need simple organizational systems that are easy to use. For organized storage of smaller toys, use under-the-bed container systems with easy-to-change labels (action heroes, doll clothes, tea party dishes, Legos, toy cars, horses, etc.). Divide toys into categories that are practical and useable.

+ Closed or semi-closed storage bins are a must. Cleaning up kids' rooms can feel like a never-ending task. The ability to toss and hide is priceless. It's fine to display a few prized items on open shelves or on the tops of bookcases and dressers, but limit the feeling of visual chaos by utilizing closed bins or baskets for most items.

+ Use a large toy box to store dress-up clothes or costumes. Inspire kids to use their imagination by making it easy to access their favorite costumes. But don't keep small items in a large toy box. It's too overwhelming, and toys may disappear, never to be found again.

+ Add bookshelves wherever you can, but also remember to keep plenty of floor space open. I like to position a bookshelf close to the bed in order to encourage reading. (Remember to safely bolt to the wall any furniture that could be a tip hazard.)

+ Create a to-do list on a chalkboard. Using chalkboard paint, you can turn just about anything into a writing surface. Kids love to write in chalk, and you can teach them the satisfaction of crossing off completed chores.

+ Once the room is set up with a place for everything, give children cleaning routines to maintain their own belongings. Incorporating a daily ten-minute "cleaning frenzy" into the before-dinner routine gives kids valuable practice in keeping a space organized and in order.

39 | INTRODUCE HOUSEKEEPING ROUTINES EARLY

Here's a motto to live by: *Simple done well is better than complicated never practiced.* If a system is too complex, you feel defeated before you even begin. And when you're teaching kids, that's even truer. Giving kids the skills to stay on top of tasks will give them the tools to succeed in any endeavor. Start young and start simple.

+ Provide age-appropriate routines along with scheduled daily cleanup times to help make maintaining order a lifelong habit.

+ Give everyone their own simple morning routine with household tasks suitable for their age or current needs. Even toddlers can help make beds, dust, or bring laundry to the hamper. Young kids can feed pets, set the table, and fold laundry.

+ Include outdoor chores. Many kids love spending time outside working in the garden, washing cars, and joining in on building projects. They're able to burn energy while learning lifelong skills.

+ Communicate your expectations clearly. For instance, show kids how much space they have available for toys or craft supplies, and tell them they can only keep what fits in that space.

+ Allow them some control. Let children help create labels for storage bins and baskets and make suggestions on how to organize. Their style might be different from yours, but they need to feel some ownership. Eventually, they'll be organizing on their own!

40 | STREAMLINE AND SIMPLIFY KIDS' STUFF

The main problem kids have with keeping their rooms clean? *Too much stuff.* Floors and surfaces covered with books, papers, and toys can overwhelm anyone. While we love giving our children a variety of options and have every intention of implementing the perfect organizational system complete with rotating boxes and bins, the reality is that too much stuff sets you back every time. I promise. You aren't a mean mom if you limit how much stuff they have to make a mess of. You're a good mom when you teach your kids to value what they have and appreciate it as well as selflessly give things away so others can enjoy them.

1. Take a critical look at the toy situation. Do your kids have so many toys within reach that they can't possibly keep them organized? Pare belongings down to only a few things your children can play with without your help and put the rest out of reach for times when you can better supervise them.

2. When my kids were younger, I put limited or even no toys or craft supplies in their bedroom. Separating out most of their toys and crafts to other spaces of the house gave the kids a sense that bedrooms were for sleeping, reading, and quiet play.

3. Don't just tell your kids to clean up their room. That's overwhelming to most kids. Show them that books go on bookshelves, stuffed animals go in their basket, and dirty clothes go in the hamper. Then when it's time to tidy, be specific. Let them know it's time to put the books away on the bookshelf so they can successfully complete the task.

4. Help kids to become orderly people. Give them their own shelves to store special things they like and inspiration boards to be creative.

5. Give them less to put away and less to clean up, and model the value of spending time together enjoying experiences over managing stuff.

6. Teaching kids the value of simplicity and being content with less when they are young will impact them in healthy ways for a lifetime.

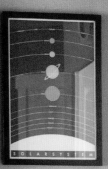

41 | ARRANGE AREAS FOR IMAGINATIVE PLAY

With just a little extra thought, you can transform a child's bedroom (or playroom) into a cozy and well-ordered retreat instead of a cavern of chaos. A room crowded with too much stuff basically guarantees a short attention span and a significant amount of frustration. Spend just a little time arranging areas for imaginative play, and watch your child's creativity flourish.

+ Divide the room into separate areas that naturally lend themselves to a certain type of activity. A doll corner, a place to play with costumes, a Lego-and-building zone, a reading nook, a special space to color and draw.

+ Think *function* when you're figuring out the separate spaces. Have zones for sleeping, reading books, and dressing, and set up each one

with what they need. Create a separate zone (in another room or designated spot within their bedroom) for toys, and another for table-type work, such as homework or crafts.

+ Toys and crafts should be organized by category and as simply as possible. Give kids buckets, bins, and baskets to store things in each designated area. Avoid complicated category labels that would be overwhelming for kids to utilize. Kids may be able to toss all of their American Girl clothes into a doll clothing bin, but if they have to separate out the doll's flannel pajamas from her winter jogging outfits, organization might end up being more frustrating than helpful.

+ Less stuff might sound like less fun for the kids, but in reality they will appreciate each toy more and may even be inspired to get a little more creative when they aren't overwhelmed and distracted by many options. Rotate the toys in each area so they can enjoy a variety of fun things and discover new surprises in the form of old favorites that have been put away for a period of time.

42 | CONTROL THE CLOTHING SITUATION

While it may seem impossible to tame the clothing monster, the same organizing principles still apply: Fewer choices and a designated home for everything. Kids grow quickly. They spill food on their clothes and get them muddy. That's natural. But you don't need to be constantly doing laundry all day, every day, or desperately trying to find a pair of pants that fits your child.

Pare down clothes. If your kids have outgrown all their school clothes, it's time to clear out the old. There is no use leaving too-small clothing items in the closet, or they might end up wearing them or being frustrated trying to find things that fit. Go through everything and give away good clothes they have grown out of. Sort through sock and underwear drawers to make sure they're stocked with clean items in the correct sizes and in good condition.

Invest in seasonal storage totes. Have a large plastic tote for each child. Dividing clothes by season (spring/summer and fall/winter) works well. While one season's clothes are in closets and drawers, the next season is waiting in the wings. You can add hand-me-down items to the container that's currently being stored.

Hop on the hand-me-down bandwagon. This is a terrific way to declutter and save money all at the same time. Resist the urge to stock up on end-of-season sales. Growth spurts are unpredictable, and what you purchase brand-new may not fit in six months or a year. Get a hand-me-down cycle going with friends. Kids love it too!

Simplify the socks. When my kids were little, we had the worst time with different colored and patterned socks losing their mates. Instead of wearing mismatched socks each day or spending precious time trying to match up all the different colors and patterns, we simplified things. We decided to just purchase one kind of white, everyday socks that went with everything. Easy solution!

43 | SET UP KIDS FOR SUCCESS IN SCHOOL

Having a well-organized study space and a full range of school supplies allow kids to develop effective study habits, work without distraction, and keep assignments and paperwork in order. All valuable tools for success in school—and life!

+ Kids feel more organized and able to get themselves ready for school if their rooms are cleared out and their belongings are streamlined. Every year kids end up with supplies and books from previous school years. Let them be involved in eliminating what is no longer needed and making space on desks and bookshelves.

+ A designated work space is a must. Start with a clear surface. Toss out any old, worn-out pens and pencils and replace with brand-new ones. Stock drawers or baskets with fresh notebook paper, printer ink, study resources, a stapler and three-hole punch, scissors and tape, and any other supplies they need.

+ Chalkboards, magnetic boards, and clipboards are great for projects, and you can use them to help kids learn to organize their own lists of assignments and deadlines.

+ A simple daily planner works well for when kids start receiving homework in class. As kids move on to upper grades, invest in a more detailed planner. They should have this down before college!

+ Corral homework, backpacks, and sport bags. The annual tradition of a new or cleaned-out backpack makes a great transition for kids to a more scheduled and organized school year. Let your kids clean out their old backpack, or if you are starting fresh, let them help pick out their new one. Get them involved in labeling everything and deciding how to organize their own school supplies and backpacks. (Note: Keep the backpacks cleaned out and maintained on a weekly basis so they retain some semblance of order and you don't lose important assignments or reminders.)

Home Office & Creative Spaces

Home Office & Creative Spaces

BRING ORDER TO
WHERE YOU WORK

When you're organizing, here's a simple formula to follow: Less stuff = more time. This is especially true in home offices and creative spaces, where papers, supplies, and chaos tend to multiply. In a matter of months, we can accumulate so much stuff that we can't find what we want, let alone see what we already have.

Making more room for what we want to do in life—and freeing up time and space to actually accomplish things—always has a positive and inspiring outcome, even if the process of letting go can feel overwhelming or impossible. When we're trying to decide what to do with the stuff or space in front of us, it's easier to choose the path of less when we remember that less is really more.

When it comes to our home office and creative spaces, we can bring order to our pursuits—be they business or imagination oriented—when we simplify our organizing methods and pare down things to the essentials. Eliminating excess paper and supplies, setting up systems that make sense, and increasing room for learning and growth put us on the path to an orderly and organized life that is inspiring and satisfying.

Space to work. Space to dream. These are goals worth working toward.

44 | TAKE CONTROL WITH A FAMILY COMMAND CENTER

Have you ever missed an important school event or family gathering? You're not alone. I've forgotten to pick my kids up from school on half days because I didn't pay attention to my calendar. I've missed their orthodontic appointments and sent my kids to school with bed heads on picture day! This is where a family command center would have come to the rescue. I've learned now that I can't live without one.

Don't overcomplicate it. Our command center is a simple magnetic blackboard we use for our most urgent papers. We locate it in the hub of our house so we don't miss the important info posted on it. You can also use a cork bulletin board, a magnetic whiteboard, or even clipboards affixed to the wall.

Keep it current and relevant. Include timely papers, calendars, invitations, to-do lists, and activity and school schedules. Use it only for urgent items that have a deadline, and get in the habit of clearing out old papers weekly. We choose not to include bills to pay. (Those have their own distinct destination.)

Include any supplies you need. As you determine what kind of system works best for your household, add any supplies. If you have a chalkboard command center, store chalk and a chalkboard eraser next to it. Magnetic canisters and cups can hold paper clips and pushpins along with pens and markers. Clips work well to hold paper and calendars. Day-of-the-week clothespins are a nice way to display important weekly reminders.

Have fun with it! You can paint the border of a boring corkboard to match your decor. Search for inexpensive add-ons to make the command center personal. The more attractive it looks, the more you'll be inclined to use it. While you're at it, add a few inspirational quotes and photos for good measure.

45 | ESTABLISH A PLACE FOR EVERYTHING

You might have an entire room devoted to crafting and hobbies, or you might have just a few shelves designated for your favorite pursuits. Some homes come equipped with a separate office or study, and in others the dining room does double duty as a work space. No matter your setup, you can organize your crafting and hobby supplies so they're easy to access and ready to go.

1. Spend as much time decluttering as you need to. If you have a lot of supplies and hobby clutter, pick just one hobby or craft category at a time to declutter and organize. While you're working on this part, be honest about what crafts and projects you have done recently. If you probably won't use it, pass it on to someone who will.

2. As you declutter, group items by category (for crafting supplies, you might have scrapbook paper, glue, glitter, gift wrap, ribbons, yarn, fabric, markers, tape, scissors, etc.). Assess what you have. You may have far more duplicate supplies on hand than you really need.

3. Test the supplies to make sure they all work (such as markers, glue, and pens). Sharpen colored pencils. Throw out anything old, broken, or ripped.

4. Organize office and craft supplies, art prints, and other smaller items in a flat drawer system to keep from losing things in deep drawers.

5. Keep a basket of "to-read" materials. This might be magazine articles, newspapers, or books—anything that will take more than two minutes of your time to read. Check the basket frequently, and pull out reading material when you have a few minutes to spare or when you're waiting for carpool pickup or during kids' activities.

6. Don't forget the details. Lining drawers with pretty paper may sound like a silly luxury when we have too much clutter to even see the paper lining the drawer. But when we get rid of things we don't need and organize what we keep, we find we are effortlessly able to indulge in little details such as happy drawers.

7. First, ask yourself if you will really use all the craft stuff you are about to organize. Take an honest look at your hobbies, goals, and schedule. If organized supplies will enrich your life and inspire you, go for it. But if a newly organized space will be filled with stuff you won't use, you should reconsider. In that case, let most of it go. Pare down to one or two simple crafts with minimal supplies and enjoy them to the full.

46 | ROTATE ITEMS SEASONALLY

Whether it's a season of the year or a season of life, you can set up a system for rotating items in your creative spaces. Better to have a simplified room that is inspiring and usable for you now, than a main living space packed to the brim with supplies for every possible occasion.

+ Contain everything! Be on the lookout for attractive bins, baskets, and boxes to make your creative space more functional. Search antique or thrift shops for vintage containers to add character to your space.

+ Save plastic totes for the things you keep in the garage or attic and rotate seasonally. Label your containers clearly on the sides so that what you need is always easy to find.

+ Transport craft supplies from one area to another with rolling carts.

+ Eliminate the bags. A drawer organizer filled with washi tape looks cuter and is much more user-friendly than a bag stuffed with washi tape and other random supplies.

+ Include a birthday bin with card-making supplies, gift wrap, ribbon, scissors and tape, and perhaps a few party gifts you've found on sale.

+ Rotate seasonal activities! Summer art project supplies—along with idea books—are perfect for those "I'm bored!" moments or overcast days. You can make a big deal of bringing out the summer bin on the first day of vacation.

+ While it can be cost-effective to buy art and craft supplies or holiday decor during after-season sales and store them in the appropriate bins, make sure you don't stock up on what you might not use. Everything we buy takes up space, even if it was on sale.

+ Be willing to give up things. If you've gone a few seasons without using something, you're probably not going to use it in the future. You may have had high hopes that you'd get into soap making when you collected all the supplies years ago, but if you haven't made more than one bar of soap in recent memory, it may be time to acknowledge it's time to pass on the supplies to someone else who will enjoy them.

47 | PARE DOWN PAPER CLUTTER

Paper clutter is a common struggle! The less paper in your life, the less you have to sort and manage. Choose paperless systems whenever possible, but beyond that, start with a paper organizing system that is easy to manage and functional rather than complicated and fancy.

Recycle it. As soon as an item comes in to your home, take care of it. If you don't need it, recycle it immediately. Keep a recycling basket handy wherever you tend to handle paper so you never have an excuse to toss items on the counter or floor.

Post it. Post important or time-sensitive stuff (such as concert tickets, sporting event passes, or restaurant coupons you intend to use) in your family command center.

Sort it. We can get inundated with tons of school papers! Sort through these every day and toss what you don't want. We use the super-simple system of taping school papers, lunch menus, and calendars to the back of the pantry door. You could use a cute bulletin board for this purpose too.

Remember it. This is especially important when it comes to bills! I keep a basket for all incoming bills (when paperless billing isn't an option). I open the bill, toss out inserts and envelopes (we pay online), and stick the paper bill in the basket. Twice a month, after I pay the bills, I put the paperwork in a "paid" file drawer, which I recycle at the end of the year.

Shred it. This one is a lot of fun! When I went on a yearlong epic paper decluttering mission, I bought a giant paper shredder and went to town. I shredded the contents of boxes filled with old receipts, bills, school papers, notes, credit cards, statements, and jumbled-up papers of the most random stuff. I recommend this method if you need to get ruthless.

File it. Get a file box or use a file drawer to set up a simple filing system for papers you may need to access in the current year. Label a folder for each category, such as tax documents; insurance documents and medical records; mortgage and car loan documents; important receipts; and warranties. Don't make your filing system too complicated. Only keep on hand what is essential in the current year. Papers you need to save longer (such as tax documents and titles) can be moved to a separate filing system.

48 | SET UP STATIONS FOR SPECIFIC TASKS

Even in a designated home office or creative space, it makes a world of difference to divide the area into special zones for maximum organization and efficiency. (Plus it's fun to decorate these spaces to inspire and delight!)

+ **Brainstorm what you need.** You might need stations for paper and mail, technology, hobbies and crafting, scrapbooking or card-making, homework and reading, or business and office tasks.

+ **Gather your supplies.** For example, in the homework zone you'll want a variety of items within reach, depending on the age of your student—books, pencils, pens, crayons, markers, calculator, bulletin board, stapler, three-hole punch, glue, tape, ruler, dictionary, paper, and highlighters.

+ **Even small areas count.** You can set up an inspiring area in your home prepared with note cards, colored pens, and stamps to send thank-you cards or notes of encouragement to friends. It doesn't take a lot of space, and it brings great rewards. You can set up space in a cabinet you love, in a pretty box with a lid, or even in a brass letter holder on your desk.

+ **Make it fun.** Arrange your area so you get maximum enjoyment while you do a dull task—such as paying the bills. In a corner of a room, I might pull up a comfortable chair to a table. I'll add some luxurious accessories, such as a soft and fluffy throw blanket to keep me warm on a chilly evening. If I will be paying bills with my laptop, I'll get my headphones so I can listen to music to make the experience even more pleasant. I'll do whatever I can think of to help set the ambience of that space so it's as comfortable as I can make it.

+ **Include the little things.** If you have space, set your favorite mug, tea bags, and a teapot or coffeemaker on a shelf or side table for an inspiring beverage break while you work or create. This helps you focus and save time. Even a pitcher of lemon water works!

DIY | WRAPPING CENTER

If you're scrambling to hunt down gift wrapping supplies each time you have a gift to give, a simple yet all-inclusive wrapping center is just what you need. Bonus: The nature of colorful papers and supplies will add a decorative accent to any area! First, consider what type of space you have available and choose one of the following:

+ A dresser

+ An unused closet

+ A back-of-the-door rack

+ A pegboard in a hallway

+ A wall rack in a spare room

+ A shelf in a laundry room

Gather everything you need, and then get creative figuring out ways to organize your supplies.

Cards and envelopes	Postage stamps
Envelopes for gift cards	Ribbons and bows
Gift bags	Rolls of gift wrap
Fold-down boxes	Scissors and tape
Pens and pencils	Washi tape

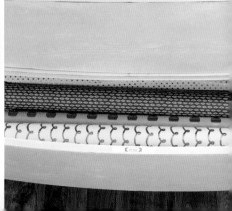

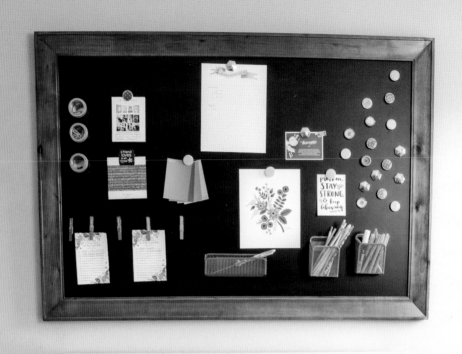

49 | FIND A HOME FOR CREATIVE SUPPLIES

In basically all households, crafting, hobby, study, and work stuff eventually end up scattered throughout different rooms. You can invest a lot of energy in picking up, or you can make some allowances for this fueled by a weekly quick cleanup session to return items to their original home.

1. If you don't have a designated room for crafts, a small basket, under-the-bed boxes, or even a secretary desk can provide space for your favorite craft or hobby.

2. Shallow drawers for crafts make it easier to keep things organized, especially small items that can easily get lost.

3. Pegboards, wall shelves, and hanging shoe organizers can maximize your vertical craft space.

4. Use labels wherever helpful to organize crafts. If you invest in a label maker, it might come in handy throughout your house!

5. Make a list of the types of activities you would like your family to be able to enjoy at home. Focus on having less random stuff, and provide more intentional opportunities to create and learn new skills through activities (such as building things, dress-up, role-playing, reading, drawing, painting, playing music or board games, cooking, doing outside exploration, etc.) to help kids (big and small) as well as grown-ups explore and develop their own talent.

6. When in doubt, invest in bookcases that offer plenty of storage space.

Conclusion

50 | EMBRACE A MIND-SET OF SIMPLICITY

If you've made it through this book, it's time to celebrate your progress. You may not have fully decluttered or organized everything in your entire home, but that's okay. Organizing is an ongoing process of simplifying your steps, creating order for the essentials, and raising your quality of living. Celebrate that you are now on a new path! With each step, you'll be developing a more fine-tuned perspective on simplicity.

As you look at your home through the lens of how *less will eventually be more*, you can more easily determine what changes *you* want to make in your home. Rather than spending time coming up with more ways to organize things you don't need, you'll more easily recognize when it's time to simply let those things go. Growing clutter and daily disorder will no longer have to be stumbling blocks.

Instead of feeling out of control and frustrated by the state of your home, you'll experience more joy in creating order. Simplicity will bring you freedom. Freedom offers you time, energy, and money to spend on what matters most to you. Organizing and housework shouldn't consume your life. Your home should be organized so that you can more fully live.

By wisdom a house is built,
and through understanding it is established;
through knowledge its rooms are filled
with rare and beautiful treasures.

PROVERBS 24:3-4

DISCOVER MORE WAYS TO DECORATE,

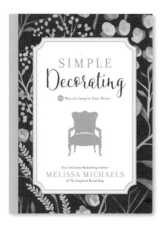

Jump-start your style and refresh your home with more than 300 practical and budget-friendly decorating tips. Let Melissa help you create a space you can't wait to come home to.

Welcoming loved ones into your home doesn't have to be intimidating when you try these affordable and inspired ideas. Learn how to host memorable get-togethers with simplicity and style.

You can love your home again when Melissa shows you how to decorate and style your rooms with ease. Dare to see your surroundings with new eyes.

DREAM, AND DECLUTTER

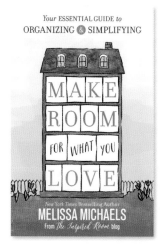

Is clutter taking over your home and life? Melissa gives you encouragement and practical advice to help you create a place for all the things you love.

Forget the rules and discover creative ways to personalize your spaces and express your style. Create a home inspired by the people, beauty, and life you love.

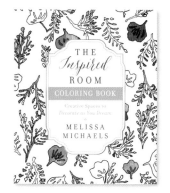

Melissa invites you to relax and unwind as you imagine the possibilities in your dream home through creative activities and beautiful coloring pages.

ABOUT THE
Author

MELISSA MICHAELS is the creator and author of the popular home decorating blog *The Inspired Room*, which inspires women to love the home they have. Since 2007 Melissa has been encouraging hundreds of thousands of readers a month with daily posts and inspiration for all things house and home. *The Inspired Room* was twice voted as the *Better Homes and Gardens* magazine Reader's Choice decorating blog.

Melissa lives with her husband, Jerry; their son, Luke; and two impossibly adorable Doodle pups, Jack and Lily, whose adventures are well loved and followed on their Facebook page (Facebook.com/jack.goldendoodle). The Michaels' daughters, Courtney and Kylee (and Kylee's husband, Lance), are an active part of *The Inspired Room*.

CONNECT WITH MELISSA AND OTHER HOME LOVERS

The Inspired Room Blog — **theinspiredroom.net**

Subscribe — Have new blog posts delivered to your inbox.

melissa@theinspiredroom.com.

Facebook.com/**theinspiredroom.fans**

Instagram

Pinterest — **@theinspiredroom**

Twitter